THE PEREGRINE FALCON

THE PEREGRINE FALCON

Alvin, Virginia, and Robert Silverstein

THE MILLBROOK PRESS • BROOKFIELD, CONNECTICUT

Cover photograph courtesy of © Mickey Gibson, Animals Animals
Photographs courtesy of U.S. Fish & Wildlife Service: pp. 6 (Mike
Smith), 20 (Dan Benfield), 23 (Karen Bollinger), 24 (Jo Keller), 55;
Animals Animals: pp. 10 (E.R. Degginger), 13 (Joe McDonald), 29
(Marty Stouffer); Dif-Vallier/Peter Arnold, Inc.: pp. 16, 17; Giraudon/
Art Resource, N.Y.: p. 28; Glen Eitemiller: pp. 32, 41, 45; UPI/Bett-
mann: p. 35; Heinz Meng, Ph.D.: pp. 38 (both), 39; Steve Allen/
Gamma Liaison Network: p. 48. Map by Joe Le Monnier.

Library of Congress Cataloging-in-Publication Data
Silverstein, Alvin.
The peregrine falcon / Alvin, Virginia, and Robert Silverstein.
p.   cm.—(Endangered in America)
Includes bibliographical references (p.   ) and index.
Summary: After reaching near extinction, peregrine falcons have
made a remarkable comeback in recent years, thanks in large to
the efforts of people determined to save them. This book presents
their story along with a wealth of information about the birds.
ISBN 1-56294-417-7 (lib. bdg.)
1. Peregrine falcon—United States—Juvenile literature.
2. Endangered species—United States—Juvenile literature.
3. Wildlife reintroduction—United States—Juvenile literature.
[1. Peregrine falcon.   2. Falcons.   3. Endangered species.
4. Wildlife reintroduction.]   I. Silverstein, Virginia B.
II. Silverstein, Robert A.   III. Title.   IV. Series: Silverstein,
Alvin. Endangered in America.
QL696.F34S55   1995   598.9'18—dc20   94-17991   CIP   AC

Published by The Millbrook Press Inc.
2 Old New Milford Road, Brookfield, Connecticut 06804

CONTENTS

A peregrine falcon, the world's fastest bird, prepares to soar.

FASTEST BIRD IN THE WORLD

The peregrine falcon is the fastest bird in the world. It can dive through the air at up to 200 miles (about 320 kilometers) per hour. Some people call it the "thunderbolt bird" because it seems as fast as lightning. Peregrine falcons are birds of prey (birds that hunt other animals) and specialize in hunting birds. Their speed helps to make them fierce hunters. They dive through the sky and snatch their prey out of the air.

Peregrine falcons can be found throughout the world, and people have admired them since ancient times. Peregrines were sacred to the ancient Egyptians, for example, and an important Egyptian god had the shape of a falcon. For thousands of years people in many cultures trained peregrines to act as hunters in a sport called falconry. Other birds of prey were also used in falconry, but peregrines were many people's favorite.

Falconry was mainly a sport for nobles, and after guns were invented even fewer people used birds of prey for hunting. Meanwhile, the average farmer or herder had a very different attitude toward peregrines. Falcons, like other birds of prey, competed with hunters for game, and they sometimes attacked farm animals such as chickens and ducks. Many people regarded birds of prey as pests and killed great numbers of them— including peregrines.

As human populations grew, people took over more and more land to build cities and industries. Wilderness areas shrank, and so did the numbers of the birds of prey that had lived in them. Large birds need huge areas to roam over in order to find enough food to survive.

Peregrines also faced other threats. Egg collectors stole peregrine eggs. Young falcons were stolen from their nests to be trained for falconry. And others were trapped in nets when they flew south for the winter. But even through all these dangers, the number of peregrine falcons remained steady in most parts of the world for hundreds of years.

Then, in the 1960s, bird-watchers noticed that peregrines seemed to be disappearing. In fact—though no one had realized it—peregrines had disappeared from the entire east coast of the United States! All over the world people were reporting decreasing numbers of peregrines.

At first scientists couldn't figure out what was happening to the peregrines. Then they slowly discovered that certain pesticides used to kill insects were also killing falcons and other birds. Other pesticides were preventing the birds from reproducing properly. Some of these pesticides were banned in many areas, but scientists worried that this action wouldn't be enough. So much damage had been done that peregrines might become extinct: There wouldn't be any peregrines left anywhere.

Programs were set up in several countries to breed peregrines and then release them into the wild. Thanks to these efforts, peregrines are once again flying on the east coast of the United States, as well as in most of the rest of the country. They can be found not only in wilderness areas but even in many large cities.

The number of peregrines has increased in many areas. But in some other places peregrines are still struggling. Harmful pesticides that are still being used in some parts of the world continue to threaten their survival. (In fact, residues of pesticides used years ago remain in places where their use is no longer permitted.) People have done much to help peregrines recover from the brink of extinction. But more needs to be done to make sure the story of the peregrine falcon will have a happy ending.

WHAT IS A PEREGRINE FALCON?

Peregrine falcons belong to a group of birds called Falconiformes, which includes eagles, hawks, and falcons. These birds are called birds of prey because they hunt and kill other animals for food.

Falcons look a lot like hawks, but their wings are longer and they curve backward, ending in a point. A falcon's wings are designed for speed, and a hawk's for soaring. Falcons have dark eyes, but hawks typically have light-colored eyes.

There are many kinds of falcons, living in varied habitats all around the world. The tiny falconets are the smallest. Some are less than 6 inches (15 centimeters) long. The gyrfalcons, found in the Arctic, are the largest falcons—nearly 24 inches (61 centimeters) long from beak to tail. In addition to peregrines, prairie falcons, merlins, and kestrels are other types of falcons that live in the United States. People have also caused the numbers of other falcons to be reduced, but they are not endangered.

THE PEREGRINE FALCON

The scientific name for peregrines is *Falco peregrinus*. Peregrine comes from a Latin word for wanderer. The birds were given this name because some peregrine falcons migrate long distances when winter comes.

Tapered wings are typical of falcons. The dark feathers at this female's eyes and cheeks are distinctive marks of the peregrine.

Peregrines are medium-sized birds, about the size of a crow. The markings of peregrines from different parts of the world are very similar. On the back and wings, most adult peregrines are slate-blue. The top of the head is black, making the bird look like it is wearing a helmet. The undersides of the peregrine's wings, tail, and chest are white, cream, or pinkish with dark bands. Black feathers around its eyes help reduce glare so the peregrine can see better. Dark feathers around its cheeks make an adult peregrine look like it is wearing a big black mustache. Young peregrines are dark brown with lots of streaks on the belly and breast. A peregrine's strong feet are yellow, with three toes in front and one in back. Each toe has a curved, razor-sharp talon.

It is hard to tell a male from a female peregrine. Both have the same color markings. But, as in most Falconiformes, the female is larger than the male. The average female weighs about 2 pounds (1 kilogram). She is 18 to 20 inches (45 to 50 centimeters) long, with a 45-inch (115-centimeter) wingspan. The female is called simply a *falcon*.

The male peregrine is called a *tiercel*, from the Latin word for a third. This name may have come from an old belief that males hatched from the third egg laid in the nest, or from the fact that the male peregrine is about one-third smaller than the female. The average tiercel is about 15 inches (less than 40 centimeters) long, and he weighs about 1½ pounds (0.7 kilogram).

AMERICAN PEREGRINES

Peregrine falcons are found all around the world, on every continent except Antarctica. There are three kinds, or subspecies, of peregrine falcons in North America. The scientific name for the American peregrine falcon is *Falco peregrinus anatum*. On the east coast it was once found throughout the eastern United States and into southern Canada. In the west it was found from California to Mexico.

Peale's peregrine (*Falco peregrinus pealei*) is found from Oregon up to Alaska and the Aleutian Islands. This is the largest of the three subspecies. The tundra peregrine (*Falco peregrinus tundrius*) is found in Alaska, Canada, and Greenland.

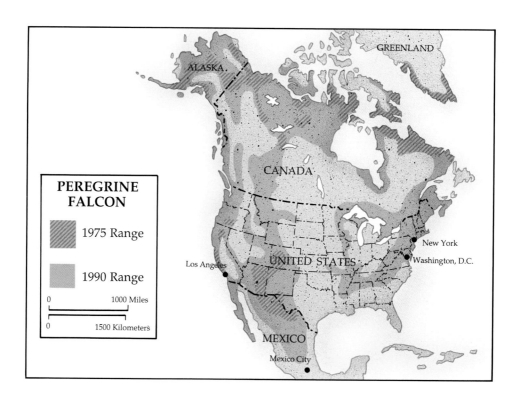

PEREGRINE FALCON

(hatched)	1975 Range
(gray)	1990 Range

0   1000 Miles

0   1500 Kilometers

GREENLAND

ALASKA

CANADA

New York

Los Angeles   UNITED STATES   Washington, D.C.

MEXICO

Mexico City

PEREGRINE HABITAT

Like most animals, peregrine falcons are usually found only where certain conditions are present. Such a place is called their habitat. The habitat of a peregrine falcon is centered around the bird's favorite perch, typically a rocky cliff that overlooks open country. The area must have plenty of songbirds, waterfowl, or pigeons that can be hunted for food. And the peregrine's nesting site is usually near a river, a lake, or the sea, because it needs to bathe often to keep its feathers clean.

A perch on a high cliff gives this peregrine falcon
a commanding view of the countryside.

Many birds build nests in trees. But the peregrine just scrapes out a hollow in the gravel or sand, high up on a rocky cliff ledge. Sometimes a pair of peregrines use another bird's nest or nests in a hollow tree or on the ledge of a building. A peregrine's nest is called an eyrie. A pair of peregrines often use the same nest year after year. Later generations may use the same nest, too. Some eyries in the United States are known to have been used for more than a century. In fact, scientists determined that a peregrine eyrie in Australia had been used for 19,000 years!

A few peregrines live in forests and make their nests in trees. These rare tree-nesting peregrines have been found in the northwestern United States, Alaska, Australia, and Sweden. (Tree-nesters in central Europe became extinct because of pesticides.)

THE WORLD'S FASTEST BIRD

In level flight falcons can reach nearly 100 miles (160 kilometers) per hour. But peregrines are famous for a kind of diving called stooping. They leap off a high perch, or climb into the sky up to 1,000 feet (300 meters), fold their wings back, and then dive down headfirst like a bullet at speeds of close to 200 miles (320 kilometers) per hour! A structure inside the falcon's nostrils helps to deflect rushing air, so that it can continue to breathe while it dives at these great speeds.

Falcons hunt during the daytime, but they are most active at dawn and dusk. When they aren't resting or hunting, they often seem to be playing. They may glide down from the sky in big loops or figure eights, or divebomb down toward the ground. Or they may glide along in a gust of wind.

FLYING SOUTH FOR THE WINTER

Peregrines can live in cold weather, but they can't live without a food supply. Many smaller birds fly south for the winter. In some areas, peregrines spend the winter near their summer home, such as in cities, where pigeons and starlings are still plentiful in the winter. But many peregrines migrate for the winter. The tundra peregrines fly the farthest of all falcons. They may fly down to the state of Florida, or to Central America or South America; some travel as much as 9,000 miles (almost 14,500 kilometers). American peregrines and Peale's peregrines do not usually go so far; they may not even migrate at all.

HUNTING FOR A LIVING

Most birds of prey swoop down to the ground to snatch up rodents or other small ground animals, but peregrines hunt mostly birds, catching them in the air. They eat pigeons, small gulls, ducks, quail, pheasants, larks, bluejays, orioles, and dozens of other kinds of birds. (Males usually hunt smaller birds than those hunted by females.) When food is scarce, peregrines may eat insects, fish, or animals that have already been killed.

Peregrines are quiet while hunting. They have good hearing and listen for bird calls. But they depend even more on their keen eyesight. Their large black eyes are set toward the front of their heads. Each eye weighs about an ounce (almost 30 grams)—this is huge in proportion to the rest of its body. If the peregrine were as big as a ten-year-old child, its eyes would each weigh several pounds!

Perched up high or soaring in the air, the falcon searches for smaller birds. When it spots its prey, the peregrine flies in pursuit. Often the chase ends with a dramatic, headfirst dive. The falcon may snatch its prey right out of the air with its razor-sharp talons and slash it quickly with its hooked beak, killing it instantly. (The beak has a toothlike notch that is used for killing prey.) Sometimes the captured bird is stunned and falls helplessly toward the ground. The peregrine may swoop down and snatch it up before it hits the ground. Or it may circle a few times and then eventually come down for its catch.

Peregrines aren't always successful in their stoops. If the smaller bird changes direction at the last moment, the peregrine will be going too fast to shift its course, and then it will have to fly back up to begin again.

After a bird has been caught and killed, the peregrine takes it to a safe spot on a cliff ledge or nearby tree, or brings it back to the nest if there are hungry babies to feed. If the prey is too heavy to carry in the air, the peregrine eats it on the ground. The feathers are plucked from the prey, and the meat is stripped off.

A peregrine's large, dark eyes are positioned toward the front to help it spot and strike the small birds it hunts. It uses the hooklike notch on its curved beak to kill prey.

A peregrine falcon grasps a jay in its powerful talons.

Peregrines have to eat a lot to stay alive, because it takes a lot of energy to hunt. They need one large or two medium-sized birds each day. Like most predators, which do not know when they will find their next meal, peregrines can gobble down huge amounts of food—as much as one quarter of their weight in a single meal! They may also hide extra food in cracks in the cliff and come back for it days later.

TERRITORIAL BIRDS

Naturalists believe that there were never a lot of peregrines in America. At most, there may have been 1,000 nesting pairs at one time. One of the reasons is that peregrines are territorial birds. Each tiercel claims an area as his own. He will drive other males away if they enter his territory. The bird's hunting range often extends about 20 miles (more than 30 kilometers) around its central roosting place. But the size of the territory varies, depending on the amount of prey in the area. If there is a lot of prey, the peregrine's home territory does not have to be as big as it would were prey scarce. Since peregrines tend to remain in the general area in which they were born, spacing out the living and hunting areas in this way helps to keep nature in balance. If too many peregrines hunted in the same area, they would quickly kill all the small birds there, or drive them away. Then there would not be enough food to support even one peregrine pair.

Peregrines live in family units of a mother and father and their chicks. They communicate with each other by calling in various ways. The tiercel makes tweeting and wailing cries when trying to find a mate. The warning cry is "cack, cack, cack." If an intruder, such as a human, doesn't listen to the warning and approaches the nest, the peregrine will defend the nest, flying right at the person.

A PEREGRINE'S LIFE CYCLE

Peregrines are able to have young when they are two years old, but they may take several years to find a mate. They go courting in the late winter or early spring. The established pairs have a courtship too, renewing their commitment for the new mating year.

The falcons that migrate for the winter return to their home territories sometime around March. Often the tiercel returns first. He marks out his territory by flying from place to place, while he calls out to other tiercels to stay away. A female may be drawn by the tiercel's call. The male performs a show for her, doing acrobatics in the sky. He soars up into the air and dives down, doing loops. The female often joins in the courtship flight. Then the tiercel may kill a bird and bring it to the falcon. He clucks softly to her.

PEREGRINES MATE FOR LIFE

If the female accepts the match, then the male will show her the eyrie he has picked out. She may take a while, searching other ledges nearby before she decides where they will make their nest. When she finds the right spot, they scrape out a hollow.

A hollow scraped in the earth makes a nest for these peregrine chicks and two eggs that have yet to hatch.

Peregrine pairs hunt and bathe together and preen each other. (Preening is using the beak to clean and rearrange feathers.) They may also touch beaks. Sharing these activities helps build up the bond that will keep them together for the rest of their lives. (If one of them dies, the widow or widower usually takes a new mate.) The female is the dominant partner in a peregrine pair.

After several weeks of courtship, they mate. The female falcon lays three or four round eggs, one at a time. They are about half the size of chicken eggs and are a cream or pink color with red or brown spots.

The eggs must be kept warm for thirty-three days and must be turned over once in a while so that they will develop properly. The female usually stays on the eggs for the entire month, taking only short breaks. The male brings food to her and may also take turns in covering the eggs.

THE CHICKS HATCH

Inside the egg a peregrine chick has its head tucked under its wing. A large muscle called the hatching muscle runs from the middle of the neck up to the top of the head. About thirty days after incubation has started, this muscle contracts. The chick's head snaps up, and a hard, pointed knob on top of the beak, called the egg tooth, hits the inside of the eggshell. This creates a pip—a small hole with tiny cracks spreading out across the shell. (The egg tooth falls off about a week after hatching.)

The chicks all begin to chirp inside their eggs. Their mother answers them with a gentle clucking. One to two days after pipping, the first chick starts to move around inside its shell. As it moves, the egg tooth saws through the eggshell. The chick turns slowly around, sawing and then resting and cheeping. After a while it has cut a ring in the shell. It rests and then pushes half the eggshell away. Then it keeps wriggling and pushing until it falls out of the shell onto its belly, completely exhausted.

A newborn chick, also called an eyas, weighs about an ounce. But in six days it will double its weight. At three weeks it will be ten times the size it was when it was born.

When the eyas breaks out of its shell, it is all wet. It does not have adult feathers but is covered instead with a coat of soft, fluffy feathers called down. The chick's head looks too big for the body, and it cannot be supported by the thin neck for very long before it flops forward. The other eggs in the nest hatch within a day or two after the first. When the eyases dry, their down is creamy white and fuzzy.

BIG APPETITES

One of the parents (most of the time, the mother peregrine) is almost always in the nest with the young chicks. They need to be protected against predators and from cold weather, rain, or snow. Parents might abandon their young for a while if a nest is disturbed. That's why it is important not to disturb a peregrine nest during extremely cold or hot weather, because the young chicks can die if they become chilled or overheated.

Peregrines are fierce hunters, but they are very gentle while caring for and feeding their young. Young chicks chirp and fuss a lot, reminding their parents that they are hungry. Peregrine parents must work hard to keep their eyases fed. At first the female almost never leaves the nest. The tiercel hunts for the whole family. When the eyases are older, both parents will have to hunt to supply all the food for the peregrine family.

The male drops food to the female, who brings it back to the eyrie. She tears off bits of meat and gives them to her chicks to gulp down. When her nestlings are small, the female plucks all the feathers off the prey before bringing it to the nest. As the falcons get older, the male begins to feed them directly, and both parents "baby" them less.

Young chicks lie sprawled out on their bellies in the nest. Or they may sit on their rear ends with their legs sticking straight out in front of them. Their parents' feet are yellow, but the young chicks have pale feet with a hint of blue. Their stomachs bulge from all the food their parents bring them. Awkwardly, they stumble around the nesting ledge, but they do not go near the edge.

Stomachs bulging with food their parents have brought, young chicks, or eyases, sit with their legs stretched out before them.

By three weeks, the first feathers start to come in on the eyases' wings and tail. Their juvenile feathers are buff- and brown-streaked. Juveniles look odd with feathers poking out through coarse down. Soon they will have mostly feathers, with only tufts of down sticking out.

As long as the parents bring plenty of food, the young falcons get along with each other. They preen each other's feathers and play games together, such as practicing attacks on sticks. But they push each other and screech for food whenever their parents approach the nest.

Bits of down remain, but this eyas has most of its first set of true feathers.

TIME TO FLY

As their feathers come in, the eyases stretch and flap their wings to build up their flying muscles. At five or six weeks old, the eyases have grown a full set of brown feathers. They are now ready to fly. Flying is an instinct; it doesn't have to be learned. But it does require a lot of practice. The eyases are born with a fear of heights that keeps them from stepping off the high cliff ledge and falling. Their parents help them to overcome this fear when the time is right.

Normally, the parents land on the nesting ledge with food for the young birds. But when the time to learn to fly grows near, the parents change the way they feed their young. A parent flies close to the ledge and drops the prey near the edge.

Soon the eyases learn to crowd around the edge whenever a parent approaches with food. They jump and push each other and squawk loudly. Then the parents tease the young by flying back and forth near the ledge with the prey, calling the chicks, to try to get them to fly.

By its fifth or sixth week of life, one of the eyases becomes impatient waiting for the food, steps off the ledge, and begins flying. Without ever learning, the young peregrine knows how to flap its wings, when to spread its tail feathers, and how to make all the other movements necessary to flying. Though a little awkward at first, within minutes the bird is flying well. It will still need a lot of practice, though, to learn how to land, how to use the winds, and all the other fine points of flying.

Soon after the first young peregrine begins to fly, the others fly too. Now they must learn to hunt. The family flies together, as if they are playing. This helps the young build their muscles and learn important skills. Parents continue to provide food for young peregrines for another month or more. They may hand prey to their youngsters while flying in the air. Or they may drop killed prey in front of the youngster, as if they are trying to teach their young how to strike birds out of the air.

While the parents are off hunting, the young practice. First they chase after falling leaves and insects. Then they chase small birds. Slowly their skills improve. Within another few weeks they are hunting on their own and no longer need their parents to catch food for them. It may take up to a year, however, before they become expert hunters.

PEREGRINE DANGERS

Peregrines can live for as long as twenty years in the wild. However, there are many dangers in the life of a peregrine falcon.

Peregrine falcons have few natural enemies. Large owls and golden eagles may kill young peregrines. Sometimes flocks of smaller birds will gang up on a peregrine to chase it away.

Accidents and diseases are an important danger for peregrines. If a peregrine doesn't land properly, or flies into an electric power line, a tree limb, or a glass window, it can be hurt or killed. When a peregrine is injured it cannot fly as well and may not be able to hunt effectively. And if it can't hunt it will starve.

Peregrines may become sick from parasites carried in birds that they eat. Lice are also a problem. Falcons take regular baths to help control lice and other pests. They bathe in a shallow river or stream, splashing around to clean off their feathers. Then they fly back to the eyrie to dry their feathers and preen them. The peregrine shakes its body and ruffles its feathers to separate them. Carefully, each feather is drawn through the beak. If its feathers become rumpled and dirty, the peregrine cannot fly well enough to hunt.

The greatest threats to peregrines, however, are humans. Egg collectors have stolen peregrines' eggs. Other people have taken their chicks to train for falconry. Angry pigeon lovers have shot them. But the most serious danger is pollution, particularly the residues of pesticides used to kill insects. Pesticides nearly drove peregrines to extinction, and their effects still threaten many peregrines around the world today.

PEREGRINES AND PEOPLE

According to ancient Egyptian myth, in the beginning of time water covered the earth until a falcon flew down through the darkness and landed on a stick that was stuck into a tiny island of dry ground. Suddenly there was light, and the waters swept back to reveal the land. Ancient Egyptians also believed that falcons brought the sun into the new day each morning. These birds thus became the symbol of eternal life and rebirth.

Falcons were sacred to the ancient Egyptians. When captive falcons died they were mummified, just like important people. One of the ancient Egyptian gods was the falcon god Horus, or Heru, which means "that which is above." Horus gave the pharaohs royal power. A falcon on a perch was a symbol for "god" even in earliest hieroglyphics.

THE SPORT OF KINGS

Falconry is the art of training falcons, hawks, and eagles to hunt game on command. Ancient Chinese and Persians were the first to develop this sport, more than three to four thousand years ago. During the Middle Ages falconry was brought to Europe, where it was called the "sport of kings."

French nobles ride out to hunt with falcons in this picture from a medieval French calendar.

A sport of patience

TO BE USED for hunting, a falcon must first be tamed—and for this falconers must have a lot of patience. First the bird has to be helped to overcome its natural fear of humans. Next it is taught to perch on the falconer's gloved hand. (A thick glove is worn for protection from razor-sharp talons.) The falconer places a hood over the bird's head when carrying it, to keep it calm. Small bells or radio transmitters are placed on its legs. These help the falconer to keep track of the bird when it flies.

Next the falcon is trained to hunt. A piece of meat is tied onto the end of a rope, and the rope is swung in a circle. The falcon learns to dive at the piece of meat. Every time it does this, it is fed by its trainer. The falcon learns that food comes from the trainer. So when it is later trained to hunt live birds, it does not fly away after catching them. It brings them back to its trainer to receive a reward of fresh meat.

A thick leather glove protects a peregrine's handler from the bird's sharp claws. Bells on the falcon's legs will help the handler track it in flight.

Over the years peregrines were generally the most popular bird used in falconry because they are the most widespread and because of their great speed. They are also gentle and easily trained—yet fierce hunters.

Falconers (people who hunt with birds of prey) sometimes took young peregrines from their nests, but these would often become too tame to hunt. Usually falconers would catch passage falcons, which are young falcons making their first migration south.

Today it is illegal to take peregrines from the wild for falconry. Peregrine-gyrfalcon hybrids, prairie falcons, and kestrels are usually used instead.

In some parts of the world, falconry is more than a sport. In Africa and Asia, nomads use the birds brought back by their trained hunting falcons as part of their diet.

A CHANGING RELATIONSHIP

After the 1600s the interest in falconry began to decrease. Guns were a much more effective tool for hunting. Some people continued the sport of falconry in Britain, the United States, and other countries. But a different relationship developed between people and peregrines. Falcons, hawks, and eagles were seen as pests in Europe, and bounties were paid for killing them. This view spread around the world, and even until recent years birds of prey were being killed in great numbers in places like the United States, Canada, Russia, and many countries in Europe. But people caused the greatest damage to peregrine falcons entirely by accident.

WHERE HAVE ALL THE PEREGRINES GONE?

Some people enjoy bird-watching as a hobby. Falcons are especially interesting birds to watch because they return to the same nest site each year. In the 1950s falcon lovers began noticing that there were fewer falcons than there used to be. They thought that the numbers of peregrines were decreasing because of human activities. People were taking over falcons' hunting territory to use for building. Other people were stealing peregrine eggs and chicks. There were scattered reports of eggs that were not hatching, and of eyries (nests) that were empty. But no one realized how big the problem was because peregrines had never been very common, and many nested far away from people.

It took some time for people to realize that peregrines were disappearing all around the world. Ironically, the discovery was made in response to a complaint that there were too *many* falcons. In 1960 a Welsh pigeon keeper spoke out on British television, urging repeal of the law protecting peregrines. He claimed that pigeon owners needed to be able to protect their expensive homing pigeons against savage peregrines, which, he said, had suddenly increased in number. A petition was filed, and the British government began an investigation. A biologist named Derek Ratcliffe was assigned to find out whether or not peregrines had increased in number and were killing too many homing pigeons.

In the late 1950s and early 1960s, a sharp decrease in the number of peregrines worldwide alerted people to the dangers that falcons faced.

Up to that point, British naturalists had thought that the peregrine population had remained fairly constant, at about 800 pairs in Britain, for hundreds of years. Falcon watchers had noted long ago that falcons tended to come back to the same cliffs to nest, year after year.

First Ratcliffe made a list of the traditional peregrine nests by checking records of falconers, bird-watchers, and egg collectors. From the records it looked as though more than 80 percent of the traditional nest sites were used each year. However, when he checked the nests during the breeding season in 1961, Ratcliffe found that less than 10 percent of the sites were occupied in southern England, and many nesting sites had been abandoned in the rest of the country, too.

The falcons that Ratcliffe did find nesting had very few young, if any at all. He also observed that many of the nests held broken eggshells that had not hatched. He and other experts had noticed this occurring more and more in the previous decade.

A survey taken in 1962 found that the situation was even worse—and it seemed to be spreading north very quickly. In fact, there were less than half the normal number of peregrines in England. Scientists estimated that at the rate peregrines were decreasing, there would be none left within five years!

Across the ocean, in the United States, scientists were gathered at an international meeting of ornithologists at Cornell University. Joseph Hickey, a biologist from Wisconsin, was at the meeting. He had published a study of peregrine nest sites two decades earlier, and had determined that there were more than 200 pairs of peregrines east of the Mississippi in the early 1940s. Someone mentioned that there was a rumor that no young peregrines had hatched on the east coast in 1962. The rumor sounded too strange to be true, but when Hickey heard about Ratcliffe's research, he and his assistants decided to examine the situation. They visited more than 130 nest sites, but could not find a single nest being used in the eastern United States. And there seemed to be many fewer peregrines in the rest of the United States, including Alaska, and in Canada, too.

It wasn't long before experts began to report that peregrine numbers were decreasing all around the world. Eventually, thirty-six countries on five continents reported a sharp decrease in the number of peregrines.

If it had not been for the mistaken claims of British pigeon lovers, the peregrine might have disappeared from the entire earth before people realized what was happening. However, even when they knew that peregrines were in danger, scientists were not sure of the cause. Was a new disease spreading through peregrines around the world?

SILENT KILLERS

Some experts began to suspect that pesticides might be involved, although they did not have any scientific proof. They knew that peregrines were doing well before World War II. And it was during the early 1940s that a whole family of synthetic insecticides was developed, the first of which was called DDT.

DDT was developed for World War II by the U.S. government, to help fight diseases spread by mosquitoes and lice that often plague troops. After the war it was released for general use, and by 1947 it was widely used. Everyone thought it was the perfect insecticide because it appeared to be completely safe for humans and, unlike other pesticides, it did not break down quickly. DDT kept on working for months or even years.

Two related pesticides, aldrin and dieldrin, were introduced in 1956 and were widely used in Britain. Soon after their introduction, though, naturalists began noticing that many wild birds were dying. In the early 1960s the use of aldrin and dieldrin was restricted, and experts reported that the peregrine population stopped decreasing in Britain. By 1967 the population actually began to increase. Some scientists, including Ratcliffe, saw this as evidence that these pesticides had played a part in the decline of peregrines in Great Britain. The poisons had built up in their bodies as they preyed on smaller birds that had eaten insects, seeds, and other plant matter sprayed with pesticides. Eventually the poison became so concentrated inside the peregrines' bodies that they died.

A helicopter blankets a field with DDT dust. In 1947, when this photo was taken, the pesticide was hailed as a perfect weapon against crop-destroying insects.

But why were the surviving peregrines having such a hard time producing young? What was causing them to lay fewer eggs, and why were the eggshells thin and fragile? The information that Ratcliffe had gathered showed that these problems had been noticed at least five years before aldrin and dieldrin were used.

Ratcliffe began to wonder whether the reproductive problems might be caused by the related, but much less toxic, pesticide DDT. He checked eggs that had not hatched in a dozen nests and found traces of pesticides—including DDE, which is the main chemical that is produced as DDT breaks down inside the body. Then he measured the thickness of the shells of eggs that were laid before 1947, when DDT came into use, and those that were laid after 1947. He found that the eggs laid after DDT use had shells that were 20 percent thinner. He also found that many other types of bird eggs had thinner shells, too.

Meanwhile, American scientists confirmed the relationship between thin eggshells and high amounts of DDE. It seemed that DDE prevented female falcons' bodies from using calcium carbonate, which is the main ingredient in eggshells. As a result, the eggshells were too thin. Some eggs were laid without any shells at all! Many eggshells broke when peregrine parents tried to hatch them. Eggs with thin shells can also lose too much moisture, causing the chick growing inside to die. With no new peregrines being hatched, there were none to take the place of older falcons that had died.

Peregrines were not the only animals affected by pesticides. Scientists around the world found that pesticides had caused the numbers of bald eagles, ospreys, and brown pelicans, as well as bats and fireflies, to decrease, too.

The chemical industry put up a strong fight to defend DDT. But the plight of the peregrine provided the scientific ammunition needed to restrict DDT and other related pesticides in the United States and Canada, and in most of Europe by the early 1970s. But some people thought this wasn't enough—simply to ban these pesticides. By the time researchers discovered the damage pesticides had been doing, peregrines were extinct in the eastern United States. The numbers of these falcons had decreased all around the world, and without help from people the species might never recover.

SAVING THE PEREGRINES

Scientists wanted to bring peregrines back to the eastern United States. But they could not just capture falcons from someplace (in the Arctic, for example, where populations were still healthy), and then release them on the east coast where peregrines had disappeared. The birds would fly back to their home or die. The only way to restore the peregrine population would be to start with chicks, which could be taught to think of the place where scientists wanted to release them as home. Then they might stay in that area to make their nests.

For thousands of years people have been capturing wild animals to tame them to live among humans. Now scientists wanted to capture and breed peregrines to release back into the wild. Many experts said it couldn't be done. Peregrines just wouldn't reproduce in captivity, they claimed. It would be impossible to provide the conditions the birds need for their special courtship flights. (In fact, some falcons trained for falconry come to think of their human owners as their mates and will not mate with other falcons.)

Heinz Meng, a biologist in New York State, believed he could get peregrines to breed. After all, falconers had worked with these birds for thousands of years, so a lot was already known about them. Meng's first effort, with a pair of peregrines captured in 1964, did not succeed. But another pair proved to be a better match.

Lancelot (left) and Guinevere mated in captivity and became the "mother and father" of breeding programs aimed at saving their species. Their first chick was Prince Philip (far right), three weeks old in this picture.

In 1967, four-week-old falcons were taken from two different locations in British Columbia, Canada. The falcons, named Lancelot and Guinevere, were placed in a special chamber that was equipped with everything the peregrines might need: perches, gravel-filled ledges, and bath pans. In 1971 they mated and produced four fertile eggs. One of the young survived and was named Prince Philip.

The next year, Lancelot and Guinevere produced four more eggs. This time the scientists removed the four eggs and placed them in an incubator. Guinevere laid five more eggs. Lancelot lived for sixteen years and Guinevere lived to the age of twenty-one, and they produced many young during their lives. About 10 percent of all the peregrines in the United States today are descended from this pair—the "mother and father" of the peregrine falcon recovery effort.

PROJECT PEREGRINE

Scientists were filled with hope when Meng was able to breed peregrines successfully. In 1970, Tom Cade and a group of his graduate students at Cornell University's Laboratory of Ornithology in Ithaca, New York, started Project Peregrine, a research program to figure out how to raise falcons in captivity. The goal would be to use these captive-bred peregrines to restore the species to places in the eastern United States.

Heinz Meng, who began the peregrine breeding program, feeds meat to young eyases.

In 1971 a long, two-story bird barn that Cornell University built for Project Peregrine was finished. The scientists called it the Hawk Barn. Peregrines were donated by Meng and other naturalists. And Cade received permission to take some Peale's peregrines from Alaska, where there were still many eyries. Cade took only one eyas from each nest he visited, so the parents would be able to raise the chicks that were left.

Four pairs of peregrines were matched up in separate apartments. But none of the pairs seemed to get along until the summer had ended and the breeding season was over. The four pairs remained together through the fall and winter. When spring came, two of the pairs courted

---

Breeding Terms

DOUBLE CLUTCHING: The first clutch of eggs is removed, and the falcon lays another clutch. A third clutch may even be laid if the second is removed. The eggs that are removed are placed in an incubator to hatch while the falcon hatches the ones that are left. This lets a female lay more eggs a year.

IMPRINTING: Like many birds, young falcons become imprinted on the caretaker that raises them. They form a bond that greatly influences the bird's development. A falcon raised by humans will not think of itself as a falcon and will not be able to breed normally. To avoid imprinting on humans, researchers used several tricks. One was to feed young peregrines with remote control models or falcon puppets.

FOSTERING: Baby chicks that hatched in an incubator are placed with adult peregrines. Scientists can even place peregrine falcon eggs in the nests of other types of birds of prey to be incubated, hatched, and raised (cross fostering).

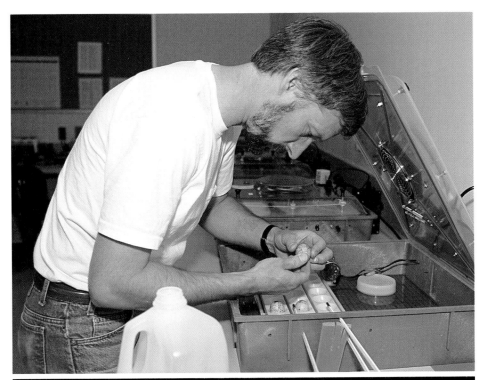

Meng's success inspired other peregrine breeding efforts.
Here a biologist checks peregrine eggs in an incubator at
the World Center for Birds of Prey in Boise, Idaho.

and mated and laid eggs. The eggs were removed from the nest so that the falcons would lay some more. The scientists had hoped to hatch the first clutches of eggs in an incubator, but none of the eggs were fertilized. The falcons laid more eggs, and one of the clutches was fertile. But the scientists were not sure about the right temperature and humidity for raising peregrines. They had set the incubator for the conditions for hatching chickens, but it was too hot and too moist; the embryos died before they could hatch.

The end of the summer had arrived, and the breeding season was over. The scientists decided to change one of the peregrine breeding matches. A male named Heyoka (this peregrine got his name—a Sioux Indian word for clown—from his habit of turning his head upside down to look at people) was not getting along with his mate. So the scientists gave Heyoka a new mate named Cadey. When spring came, Cadey and Heyoka courted and mated, and Cadey laid a clutch of four eggs.

Cadey was upset when the scientists took her eggs, but a few weeks later she laid four more. These too were removed, and then she laid another four. Soon the first clutch had hatched. The new eyases were cared for by the scientists for two weeks. Then they were placed back in the nest with Cadey and Heyoka, and the third clutch of eggs was taken to be incubated. During that summer three of the four peregrine pairs laid fertile eggs, and twenty-two chicks were hatched in the incubator. Twenty lived to learn to fly in the bird barn. In 1974, Project Peregrine was even more successful. Five breeding pairs produced twenty-three chicks.

The breeding part of the project was a complete success. Eventually, Project Peregrine was able to raise as many as two hundred peregrines a year. But breeding was only half the battle. The scientists still wanted to reintroduce peregrines into the wild.

RETURN TO THE WILD

Once it was known that peregrines could be bred in captivity, a recovery plan was quickly set up. A list of suitable sites for reintroducing peregrines in the eastern United States was drawn up. When the Endangered Species Act was passed in 1973, peregrine falcons were added to the list of endangered species. This law would then give the peregrines full protection when they returned to the wild. An information program that would gain support from and educate people about the recovery plan was also set up.

GETTING READY

Scientists had to figure out the best way to reintroduce falcons into the wild. Young falcons have to learn how to find food and protect themselves from predators. Fortunately, a lot of the peregrine's hunting behaviors are instinctive.

Peregrines were prepared for survival in the wild by adapting a falconry method called "hacking." Young falcons are given some freedom but are fed by their captors. They slowly become less dependent on people, and eventually they are able to feed and fend for themselves when it is time for them to be set free. A falcon is hacked in the area where it will be released so that it will become used to its surroundings. Then it is more likely to come back to this same area, just as wild birds come back to the same nesting site year after year.

Before a peregrine is old enough to fly, it is placed in a "hack box." Food is placed in the box each day. When it can fly, the bird is allowed to leave the box. But since it is just beginning to fly, it cannot go very far, and it returns to the hack box to be fed. For about six weeks the falcon continues to return to the hack box. (This is how long it takes a young falcon to mature in the wild.) Then the box is closed, and food is no longer provided. The falcon is free to live and hunt on its own.

BACK TO THE WILD

In 1974, Project Peregrine released the first captive-bred peregrine falcons into the wild. Two peregrines were placed in the nest of a pair of peregrines in Colorado whose own eggs had failed to hatch, and two were released off a building on the campus of the State University of New York at New Paltz, in collaboration with Heinz Meng. Over the years other groups in the United States and in other countries around the world began to breed and reintroduce peregrines. By the early 1990s more than 4,300 peregrine falcons had been set free all across America. Many were released in countries such as Canada, Germany, and Sweden, too.

Life is hard in the wild. Only about half of the peregrines that learn to fly make it to their first birthday. Even fewer reach maturity the next year. This is true both for wild falcon populations and for the captive-bred birds that are reintroduced. That is why many captive-bred peregrines must be released into the wild to establish a single new breeding pair. But

A young peregrine falcon in a hack box.

Groups Helping Peregrines

WHILE BREEDING peregrines at Cornell, Tom Cade set up a separate Peregrine Fund to seek public support for restoring peregrines. In 1974 the Colorado Division of Wildlife asked Cade to set up a Rocky Mountain Peregrine Breeding Program. Then, in the late 1970s, another peregrine breeding and restoration program was set up at the University of California, Santa Cruz.

In 1984 the Peregrine Fund expanded its focus when it opened the World Center for Birds of Prey in Boise, Idaho. The goal of the World Center includes programs of research, public education, and the breeding and reintroduction of many types of birds of prey around the world.

the release programs are working. When the programs were first begun in the mid-1970s, there were only sixty known nesting pairs of peregrines in the lower forty-eight U.S. states. But by 1993 there were close to eight hundred pairs of American peregrines, including about seventy-five pairs breeding in cities.

PEREGRINES IN CITIES

By the late 1970s the first chicks had hatched in the wild from peregrines that had been bred in captivity. Many of the birds returned to eyries in the wild that had been empty for decades. But other peregrines made their nests in cities. Skyscrapers or bridges make perfect nesting sites. They are similar to mountain ledges on which the falcons nest in the wild. Tall buildings allow the peregrine to dive down to snatch up pigeons, blue-jays, sparrows, and other small birds at any time of year.

Falcons are not new to cities. Before the peregrines disappeared from the east coast, some had moved into cities such as New York City on their own. People had mixed feelings about them in the early part of this century. Those who loved pigeons and songbirds thought of peregrines as vicious killers. Some city residents were afraid that these large birds of prey could be dangerous to humans. The media often played on this fear. New York papers, for example, printed sensational stories about per-egrines attacking humans, or described huge, gory pigeon massacres.

But in some cities peregrines were encouraged to nest and breed. In Montreal, for example, a pair of peregrines tried to lay their eggs on a skyscraper in 1937, but the eggs rolled down a drainpipe. Falcon watchers filled a large tray with gravel and hung it from one of the ledges. The peregrines returned to the man-made nesting ledge each year, and between 1940 and 1952 they raised more than twenty chicks.

Today there are peregrines living in about fifty cities across the United States (including Baltimore, Chicago, Cincinnati, Denver, Detroit, Los Angeles, Minneapolis, New York City, Philadelphia, San Diego, San Francisco, and Washington, D.C.), as well as in cities in other countries around the world. Most were either released by people or are descended from birds that were. As Tom Cade says, "No one expected urban per-egrines to be as successful as they have been."[1]

Living in cities presents many dangers for peregrines, however. Because buildings and other structures are crowded together, it is easy for the birds to accidentally crash into a building or smokestack. Windows are especially dangerous because the birds may not see the glass and crash into them. While there may not be any great horned owls to worry about, city peregrines have to dodge helicopters. People have to make accom-

Peregrine falcons have learned to live in New York and
other cities, nesting on skyscrapers instead of cliffs.

modations, too. Building and bridge maintenance crews have to work around the peregrines without disturbing them too much. Even window washers have to be careful. At some buildings, window washers are attacked so often during the breeding season that the windows are left unwashed for a few months until the young peregrines have left the nest.

In many cities people go out of their way to make peregrines feel welcome. In 1993, for example, the city of Cleveland was preparing for its annual Fourth of July fireworks display, which takes place at a skyscraper called Terminal Tower, when two eggs were found in a peregrine nest on the building. The show promoters worked with city officials and the police and fire departments to move the fireworks to a nearby parking lot. A laser show featuring an image of a flying falcon was added to the program, and the orchestra played "Rock-a-Bye Baby" while 100,000

Peregrine Romance Stories

PEREGRINES that are bred in captivity are banded—fitted with an identification band fastened around the leg like an ankle bracelet—before they are released. Falcon watchers around the United States can observe and keep track of their activity. There have been many "romantic" stories about peregrines released into the wild. A male may wander great distances to meet a female who has also traveled far from where she was released. They pair up and settle down, in a city or in the wild. A falcon released in Toronto, Canada, for example, flew to Toledo, Ohio, where it met a falcon that had been released in St. Louis, Missouri. The two falcons raised their young on a tall building in Toledo.

spectators joined in the lullaby for the falcons. The male falcon stayed on the nest throughout nearly the entire show. Two days later, the chicks hatched and were appropriately named Stars and Stripes.

RESTORING FALCONS ON THE WEST COAST

The restoration program on the west coast was a little different from the one in the east. Some peregrines were still left in the wild. Until 1950 there were about three hundred nesting pairs in California. But the number dropped drastically during the early 1960s, and by 1970 only two nesting pairs could be found.

The Santa Cruz Predatory Research Group has worked to restore peregrines across the western United States. In addition to hacking, a process called augmentation is used in the west coast program and elsewhere. Thin-shelled eggs that probably would not hatch on their own are taken from the wild and hatched in an incubator. (Cracked eggs are patched with glue and coated with wax so that the eggs will not dry out.) Later the chicks are placed back in the nests for the wild parents to raise.

Since peregrines nest on high, steep cliffs, getting to their nests is often rather difficult, requiring a skilled patient rock climber. When the climber comes close to the nest, the peregrine parents will screech and swoop down, trying to defend their eggs. Carefully, the climber must place the fragile eggs in a padded box. Then he or she places special plastic or plaster eggs into the nest to trick the parents. The falcons will sit on these plastic eggs, mistaking them for their own. The naturalists want to keep the peregrines interested in the nest site and ready to care for their young: About three weeks after the fragile eggs have hatched in the laboratory, the young falcons will be returned to the nest. The parents hardly seem to realize that their eggs have suddenly become hungry young chicks.

———

It isn't only experts that have helped peregrine falcons to make such a dramatic comeback. Volunteers all around the world have helped to band peregrines and monitor nesting pairs. However, the peregrine's very popularity can be hazardous. Falcons, like other animals, breed only at certain times of the year. If too many well-meaning observers disturb them at critical times during the nesting season, the falcons might not be able to breed properly that year.

Some other people harm peregrines on purpose. Even though the birds are protected by law, reports are still heard of peregrines that have been killed by pigeon lovers and others who disapprove of recovery efforts.

THE FUTURE OF PEREGRINES

Thanks to the programs set up by concerned people, peregrines have made a dramatic comeback from the brink of extinction. The population in many places had recovered so well that some scientists suggested that the American peregrines in the lower forty-eight U.S. states be downlisted to "threatened," instead of "endangered." This means that they are no longer in immediate danger of becoming extinct, but are still threatened with extinction if they do not receive some protection. (The Endangered Species Act provides protection for threatened species, but not as much as for endangered species.)

However, although peregrines have nearly completely recovered in some areas, they are still struggling in others. In much of the west—for example, Arizona, New Mexico, and Colorado—peregrines are no longer in danger of extinction. But along the Pacific coast (California, Oregon, and Washington) and in the northern Rockies, they are still struggling for survival. Some scientists believe that peregrines should be listed on a region-by-region basis. (This is how grizzly bears are listed.) But for now American peregrines will remain as "endangered" because the overall population of peregrines is still low. The U.S. Fish and Wildlife Service currently lists a species region by region only if scientists can show that there is a unique subspecies found in each region.

Since the Arctic peregrines that nest in Alaska, Canada, and Greenland are a separate subspecies (the tundra peregrines) and are now doing very well, the Fish and Wildlife Service proposed in 1993 to remove them from the list of endangered animals. In the early 1970s there were only about two thousand of these peregrines left, and they were listed as a threatened species. But by early 1992 it was estimated that there were five thousand to ten thousand Arctic peregrines. "Here is real evidence that the Endangered Species Act does what it was intended to do—bring back species from the brink of extinction," declared Mollie Beatie, director of the Fish and Wildlife Service.[2]

THE PROBLEM THAT WON'T GO AWAY

In many areas falcons have recovered so well that re-introduction programs have been stopped. However, peregrines in these areas will still need attention for many more years to make sure the small populations in places like New York State remain healthy. They must be carefully watched and protected. Nest boxes at city eyries have to be built and kept up. Bridge and building maintenance must be done without disturbing falcons.

In other areas, scientists are still working hard to help falcons. They are frustrated because, twenty years after DDT was banned, there are still many places where peregrines are having reproductive problems. In Big Sur, California, scientists are able to hatch only 40 percent of the eggs taken from the wild because they are so contaminated with DDE and other chemicals. Workers must even wear gloves when handling the eggs because materials in the eggs are often highly toxic.

The problem at some places, such as Big Sur, is due to "hot spots" of contamination. Chemical companies dumped hundreds of tons of DDT into the oceans off the coast of southern California in the 1950s and 1960s. One plant dumped nearly 600 pounds (270 kilograms) a day! The contamination of Big Sur eggs has remained high over the years, and lately new pollutants such as dioxins are being found in them. Scientists suspect that some of these pollutants may be responsible for the eggs that do not hatch.

The other part of the problem is that, even though the use of DDT and other dangerous pesticides is banned in the United States, companies are allowed to manufacture them and export them to other countries. Today these pesticides are still used in Central and South America, Africa, and India. No one really knows how much DDT is being used on farms, forests, and swamps in the world. Although the amount has been decreasing, the numbers are still alarming. In Mexico, for example, 9 million pounds (about 4 million kilograms) of DDT were being used each year in the early 1990s.

In the autumn, peregrines from the north head south for the winter, and many fly to places where DDT is still used. Many smaller birds do too. When they return, having accumulated DDT in their body tissues from eating contaminated grains and insects, they may in turn be eaten by peregrines. This is the reason why peregrines in cities often fare better than peregrines in wilderness areas. City peregrines eat mostly pigeons, which have little DDT contamination.

A LESSON TO BE LEARNED

Many environmentalists point out that the lesson the peregrine story should have taught us is that people cannot use so many pesticides and

The comeback of the peregrine falcon is an environmental success story, but these magnificent birds still need protection in many areas.

other chemicals without producing potentially dangerous changes in our world. Each year nearly 23 million tons of pesticides are dumped on our planet. How many other species of animals and plants are being affected by chemicals like DDT? How will these environmental pollutants affect humans? Tom Cade calls peregrines "a unique biological monitor of the quality of the world's environments."[3]

Besides killing certain species of animals and plants or causing reproductive problems, pesticides can also have less direct effects by changing the whole ecosystem of an area. Herbicides that kill weeds, for example, may be completely nontoxic, but they change the habitat, making less food for insects. A decrease in the number of insects means less food for birds. This is what caused the grey partridge to experience a population crash in the British Isles.

Today there are nearly 1,400 pairs of American peregrines and 4,000 pairs of peregrine falcons in Europe. This is four times as many as there were twenty years ago. The story of the peregrine's comeback from the verge of extinction is one of the greatest endangered animal success stories. But it is still being written.

NOTES

1. Steven E. Levingston, "In Urban Canyons, Peregrine Falcons Are Thriving Again," *Wall Street Journal*, October 7, 1993.

2. Associated Press, "Raptor's Revival: Falcon May Be Removed From Danger List," *The New York Times*, October 12, 1993.

3. Galen Rowell, "Falcon Rescue," *National Geographic*, April 1991.

FURTHER READING

Arnold, Caroline. *Saving the Peregrine Falcon*. Minneapolis: Carolrhoda Books, 1985.

Green, Carl R., and William R. Sanford. *The Peregrine Falcon*. Mankato, Minnesota: Crestwood House, 1986.

Savage, Candace. *Peregrine Falcons*. San Francisco: Sierra Club Books, 1992.

Schick, Alice. *The Peregrine Falcons*. New York: Dial Press, 1975.

Wallace, David Rains. *Life in the Balance*. New York: Harcourt Brace Jovanovich, 1987.

ORGANIZATIONS

Defenders of Wildlife
1244 Nineteenth Street, NW
Washington, DC 20036
(202) 659-9510

Hawk Watch International
P.O. Box 35706
Albuquerque, NM 87176-5706
(505) 255-7622

National Audubon Society
950 Third Avenue
New York, NY 10022
(212) 832-3200

The Peregrine Fund, Inc.
5666 West Flying Hawk Lane
Boise, ID 83709
(208) 362-3716

Pesticide Action Network
North American Regional Center
965 Mission Street #514
San Francisco, CA 94103
(415) 541-9140

Rocky Mountain Raptor Program
Veterinary Teaching Hospital
Colorado State University
300 West Drake
Fort Collins, CO 80523
(303) 491-0398

U.S. Fish and Wildlife Service
Department of the Interior
Washington, DC 20240
(202) 208-5634

FACTS ABOUT PEREGRINE FALCONS

Size*   Female: 18 to 20 inches (about 45 to 50 centimeters) long, 45-
                          inch (115-centimeter) wingspan
                 Male: 15 inches (under 40 centimeters) long, 41-inch (105-
                          centimeter) wingspan

Weight*   Females: about 2 pounds (1 kilogram)
                 Males: about 1½ pounds (0.7 kilogram)

Color   Top of head black, back and wings slate-blue, underparts white,
                 cream, or pinkish with dark bands; dark feathers around eyes and
                 cheeks

Food   Pigeons, small gulls, ducks, quail, pheasants, larks, bluejays,
                 orioles, and other small birds

Reproduction   Breed every spring starting at 2 years old; lay 4 or 5 speckled eggs;
                 hatching about 33 days

Care for young   Female sits on the eggs nearly full-time; male feeds her and may
                 briefly sit on eggs; after hatching, female remains at nest and male
                 brings food; later both parents continue to feed chicks (eyases)
                 until they are 2 months old

Range	American peregrine:	Various parts of the United States (lower 48 states and Alaska) and Canada
	Peale's peregrine:	Canada and Alaska (mainly Queen Charlotte and Aleutian Islands)
	Arctic (tundra) peregrine:	Breeding range in Canada, Alaska, and Greenland; migrates for the winter to Florida, Mexico, Central America, or South America

Peregrine falcons are also found in parts of Europe, Asia, Africa, and Australia

Population size	American:	about 2,800
	Peale's:	about 1,700
	Arctic (tundra):	about 4,000 to 10,000
Social behavior	Usually mate for life; migrating peregrines stay together in pairs and return to the same nest each spring	
Life span	About 20 years	

*Size varies depending on the subspecies. Sizes given are for the American peregrine; Peale's and tundra peregrines are somewhat larger.

INDEX

Page numbers in *italics* refer to illustrations.

ABOUT THE AUTHORS

Alvin Silverstein is a
professor of biology at the
City University of New York,
College of Staten Island;
Virginia Silverstein, his wife,
is a translator of Russian scientific literature. Together they
have published nearly 100 books
on science and health topics.

Robert Silverstein joined his
parents' writing team in 1988
and has since co-authored more
than a dozen books with them,
including the Food Power nutrition
series from The Millbrook Press.